Broadway Classics
FOR Ukulele

Arranged by Jim Beloff

ISBN 978-1-4584-1565-3

HAL•LEONARD®
CORPORATION
7777 W. BLUEMOUND RD. P.O. BOX 13819 MILWAUKEE, WI 53213

Visit Hal Leonard Online at
www.halleonard.com

Contents

Any Dream Will Do

from JOSEPH AND THE AMAZING TECHNICOLOR® DREAMCOAT

Music by Andrew Lloyd Webber
Lyrics by Tim Rice

gold - en coat flew out of sight. __ The col - ours fad - ed

in - to dark - ness, I was left a - lone. _____

Verse

N.C.

3. May I re - turn to the be -

gin - ning, the light is dim - ming and the dream is

too. The world and I, we are still wait - ing,

still hes - i - tat - ing, an - y dream will do,

Outro

an - y dream will do, an - y dream will do.

Baubles, Bangles and Beads

from KISMET
Words and Music by Robert Wright and George Forrest
(Music Based on Themes of A. Borodin)

First note

Chorus
Moderately

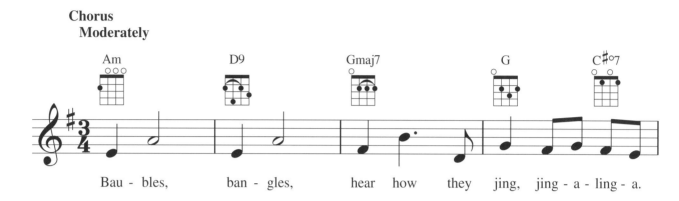

Bau - bles, ban - gles, hear how they jing, jing - a - ling - a.

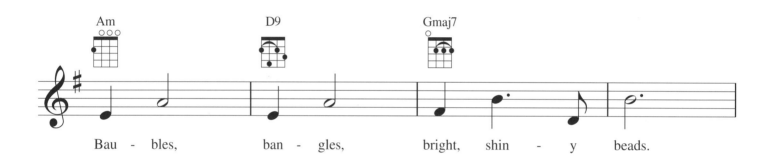

Bau - bles, ban - gles, bright, shin - y beads.

Spar - kles, span - gles, my heart will sing, sing - a - ling - a,

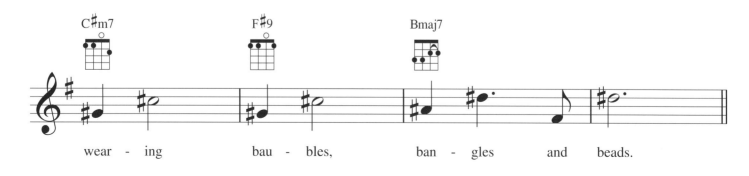

wear - ing bau - bles, ban - gles and beads.

Bridge

I'll glit - ter and gleam so,

make some - bod - y dream so, that

Outro-Chorus

some - day he may buy me a ring, ring - a - ling - a.

I've heard that's where it leads, _____

_____ wear - ing bau - bles, ban - gles and

beads. _____

7

Bewitched

from PAL JOEY
Words by Lorenz Hart
Music by Richard Rodgers

of it? He is cold, I a - gree.

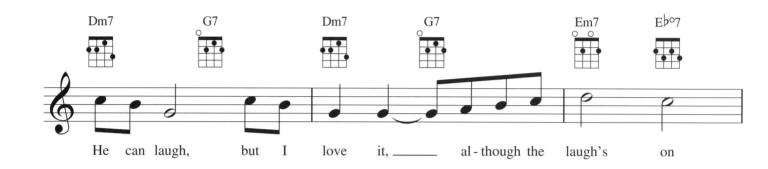

He can laugh, but I love it, _____ al - though the laugh's on

Outro-Chorus

me. I'll sing to him, each spring to him, and

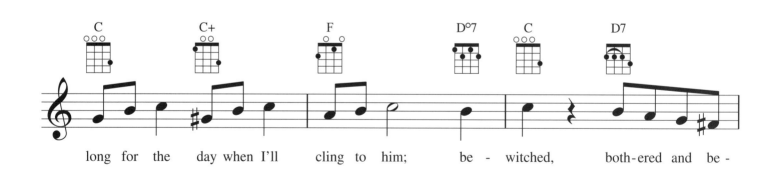

long for the day when I'll cling to him; be - witched, both - ered and be -

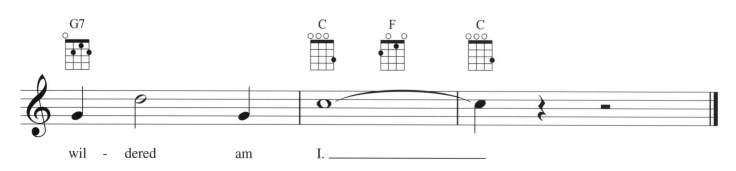

wil - dered am I. _____

Big Spender

from SWEET CHARITY
Music by Cy Coleman
Lyrics by Dorothy Fields

First note

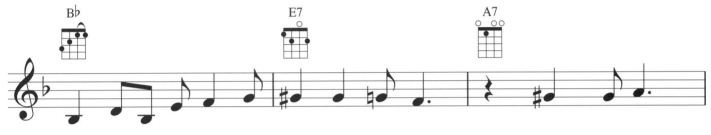

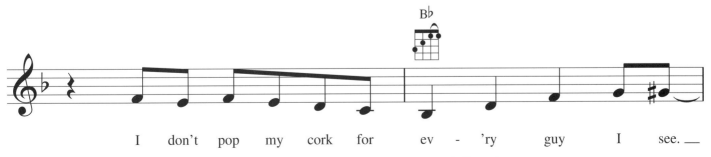

Hey! Big spend - er! Spend

a lit - tle time __ with me.

Bridge

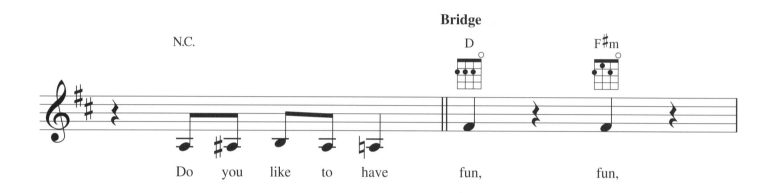

Do you like to have fun, fun,

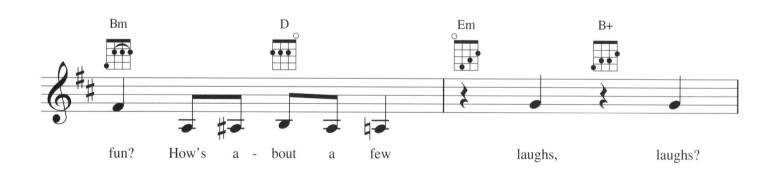

fun? How's a - bout a few laughs, laughs?

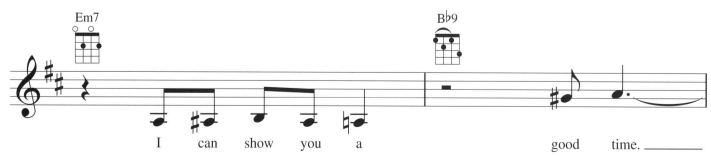

I can show you a good time. _____

Let me show you a good time. _____ The min-ute you

Coda

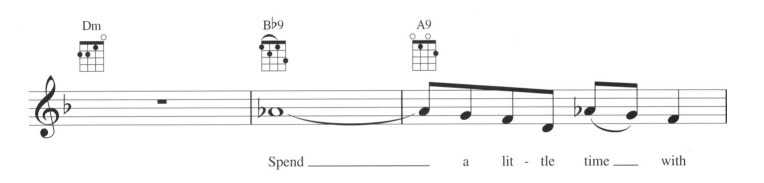

Hey! Big spend - er! Hey! Big spend - er!

Spend _____ a lit - tle time ____ with

Outro

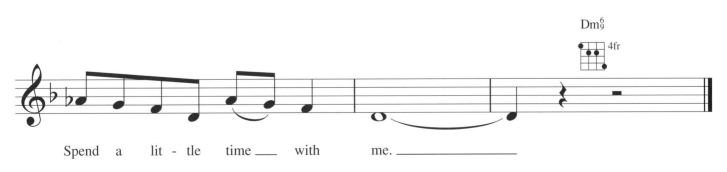

me. Spend a lit - tle time ____ with me.

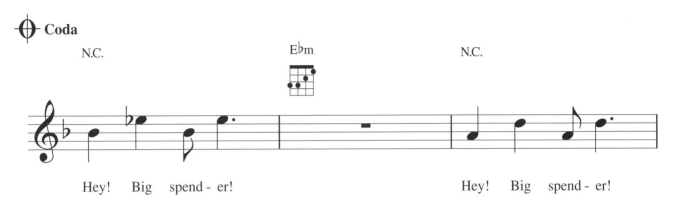

Spend a lit - tle time ____ with me. _____

A Bushel and a Peck

from GUYS AND DOLLS
By Frank Loesser

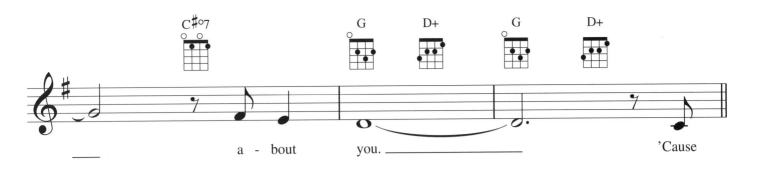

a - bout you. _____ 'Cause

Chorus

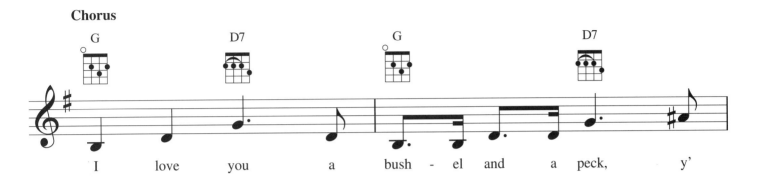

I love you a bush - el and a peck, y'

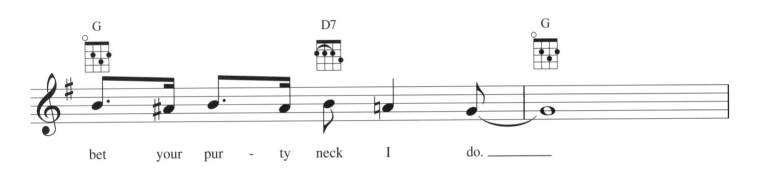

bet your pur - ty neck I do. _____

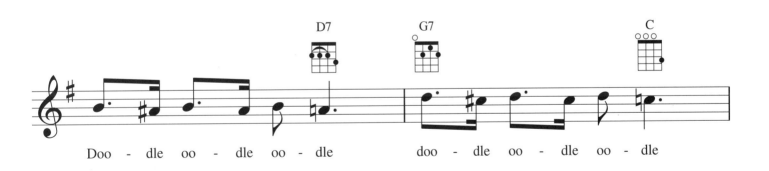

Doo - dle oo - dle oo - dle doo - dle oo - dle oo - dle

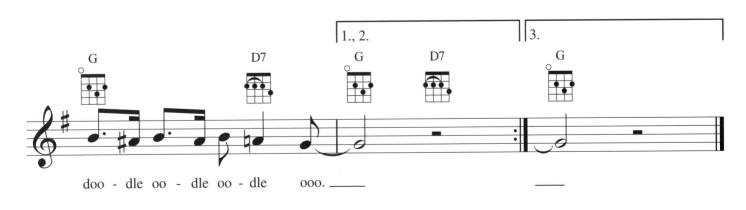

doo - dle oo - dle oo - dle ooo. _____

Cabaret

from the Musical CABARET
Words by Fred Ebb
Music by John Kander

First note

Chorus
With vigor

1. What good is sit - ting a - lone in your room? ___
2. Put down the knit - ting, the book and the broom; ___
3. No use per - mit - ting some proph - et of doom ___
4. Start by ad - mit - ting, from cra - dle to tomb, ___

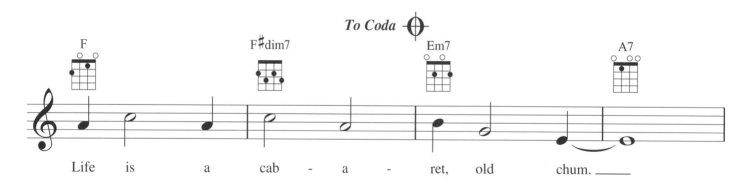

___ Come hear the mu - sic play. ___
___ time for a hol - i - day. ___
___ to wipe ev - 'ry smile a - way. ___
___ it is - n't that long a stay. ___

To Coda ⊕

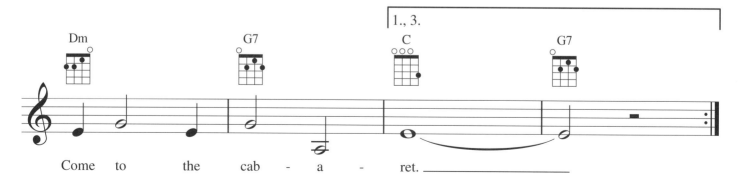

Life is a cab - a - ret, old chum. ___

1., 3.

Come to the cab - a - ret. ___

ret.   Come taste the wine,

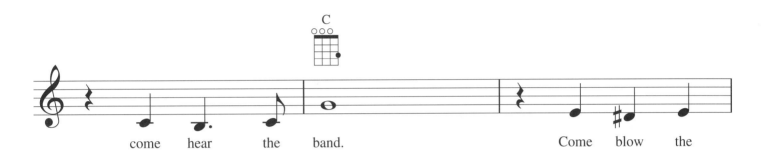

come hear the band.   Come blow the

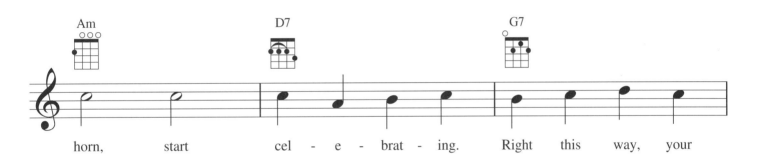

horn, start cel - e - brat - ing. Right this way, your

Coda

D.C. al Coda
(take 2nd ending)

Outro

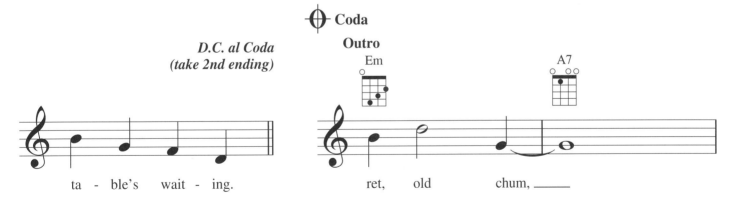

ta - ble's wait - ing.   ret, old chum, _____

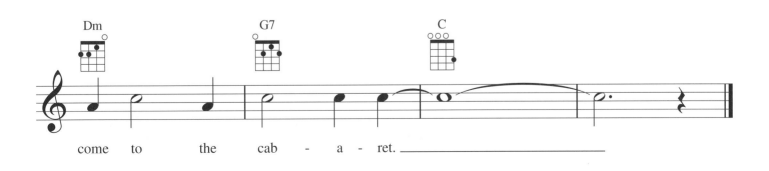

come to the cab - a - ret. _____

Can't Help Lovin' Dat Man

from SHOW BOAT
Lyrics by Oscar Hammerstein II
Music by Jerome Kern

A Cockeyed Optimist

from SOUTH PACIFIC
Lyrics by Oscar Hammerstein II
Music by Richard Rodgers

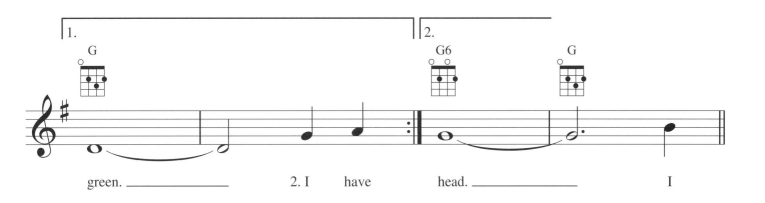

green. _____   2. I have   head. _____   I

Bridge

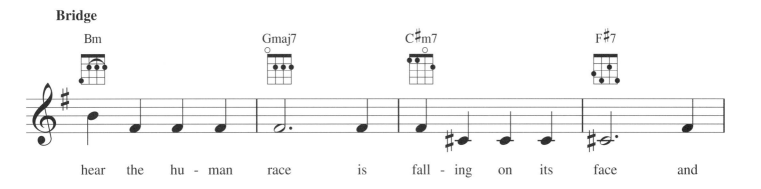

hear   the   hu - man   race   is   fall - ing   on   its   face   and

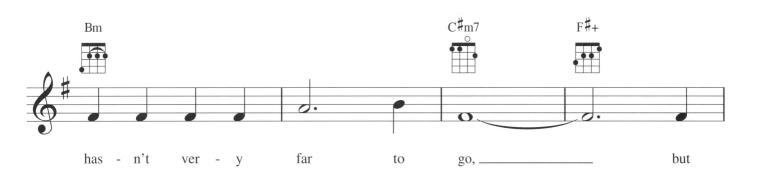

has - n't   ver - y   far   to   go, _____   but

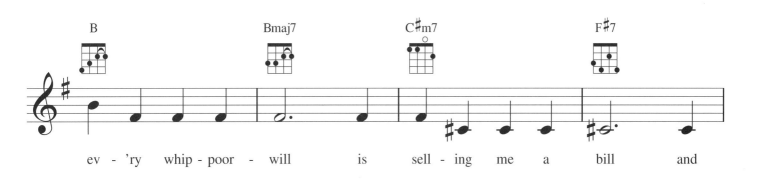

ev - 'ry   whip - poor - will   is   sell - ing   me   a   bill   and

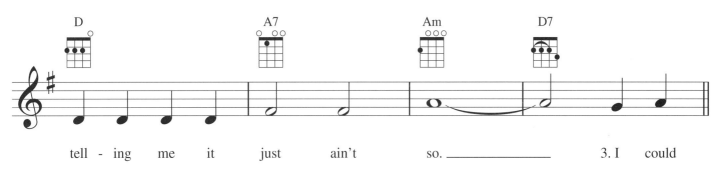

tell - ing   me   it   just   ain't   so. _____   3. I could

Verse

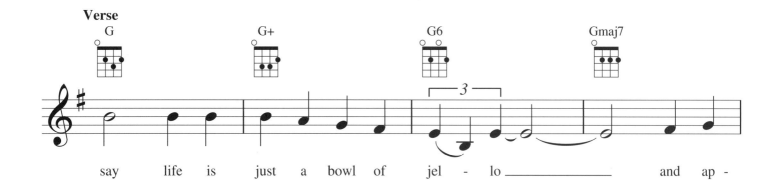

say   life   is   just   a   bowl   of   jel - lo _____ and   ap -

pear   more   in - tel - li - gent   and   smart, _____   but   I'm

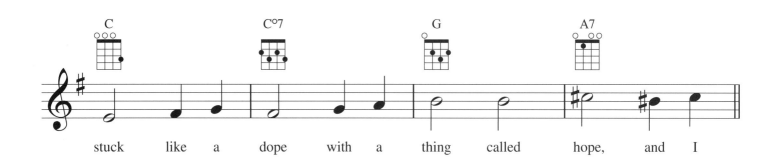

stuck   like   a   dope   with   a   thing   called   hope,   and   I

Outro

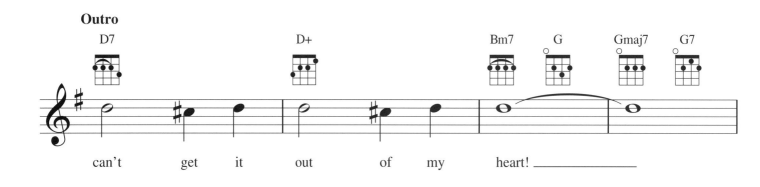

can't   get   it   out   of   my   heart! _____

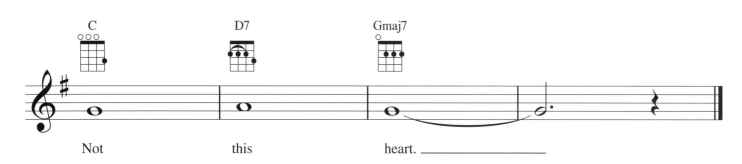

Not   this   heart. _____

22

Blue Skies

from BETSY
Words and Music by Irving Berlin

1. Blue skies _____ smil-ing at me, _____
2. Blue - birds _____ sing-ing a song, _____
3. Blue days _____ all of them gone, _____

____ noth-ing but blue skies _____ do I see. _____
____ noth-ing but blue - birds _____ from now on. __
____ noth-ing but blue skies _____ from now on. __

Bridge

Fine

Nev-er saw the sun shin-ing so bright,

nev-er saw things go-ing so right. No-tic-ing the days

D.C. al Fine

hur-ry-ing by, when you're in love, my how they fly.

Come Rain or Come Shine

from ST. LOUIS WOMAN
Words by Johnny Mercer
Music by Harold Arlen

Consider Yourself

from the Broadway Musical OLIVER!
Words and Music by Lionel Bart

on   the   house! _____   Con -

Outro-Chorus

sid - er   your - self _____   our   mate. _____

_____   We   don't   want   to   have _____   no

fuss. _____   For   af - ter   some   con -

sid - er - a - tion,   we   can   state: Con -

sid - er   your - self _____   one   of   us. _____

Easter Parade

from AS THOUSANDS CHEER
Words and Music by Irving Berlin

First note

Chorus
Moderately

1. In your Eas - ter bon - net, with all the frills up -
2. I'll be all in clo - ver, and when they look you
3. I could write a son - net a - bout your Eas - ter

on it, you'll be the grand - est la - dy in the
o - ver, I'll be the proud - est fel - low in the
bon - net and of the girl I'm tak - ing to the

1.

Eas - ter Pa - rade.

2., 3.

Eas - ter Pa - rade. On the

Fine

Bridge

F9   Bb6

Av - e - nue,   Fifth Av - e - nue,   the pho-

D.C. al Fine
(take 2nd ending)

to-graph-ers will snap us, and you'll find that you're in the ro - to - gra - vure. Oh,

Gonna Build a Mountain

from the Musical Production STOP THE WORLD – I WANT TO GET OFF
Words and Music by Leslie Bricusse
and Anthony Newley

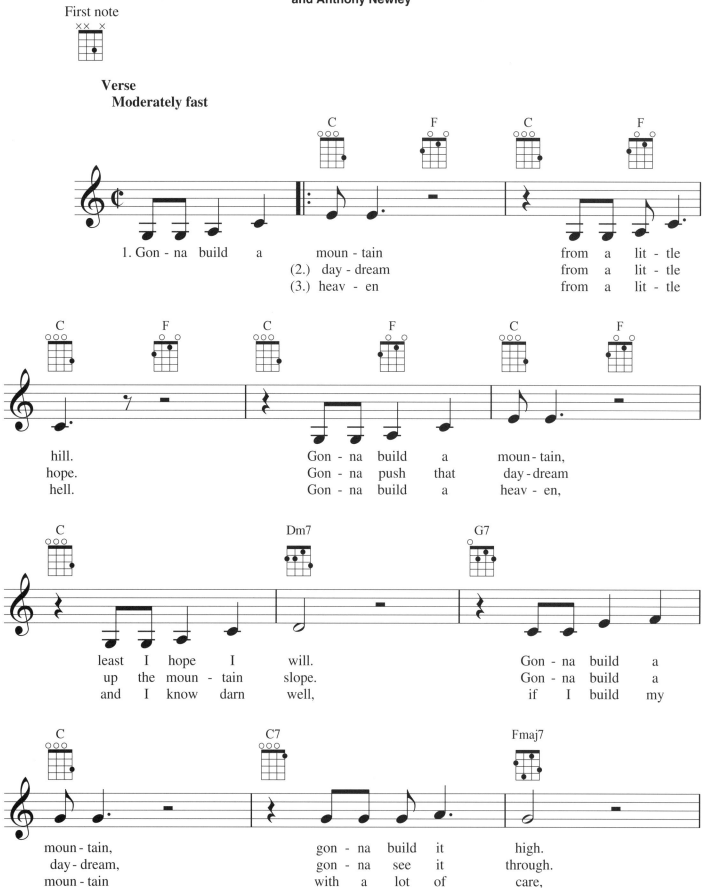

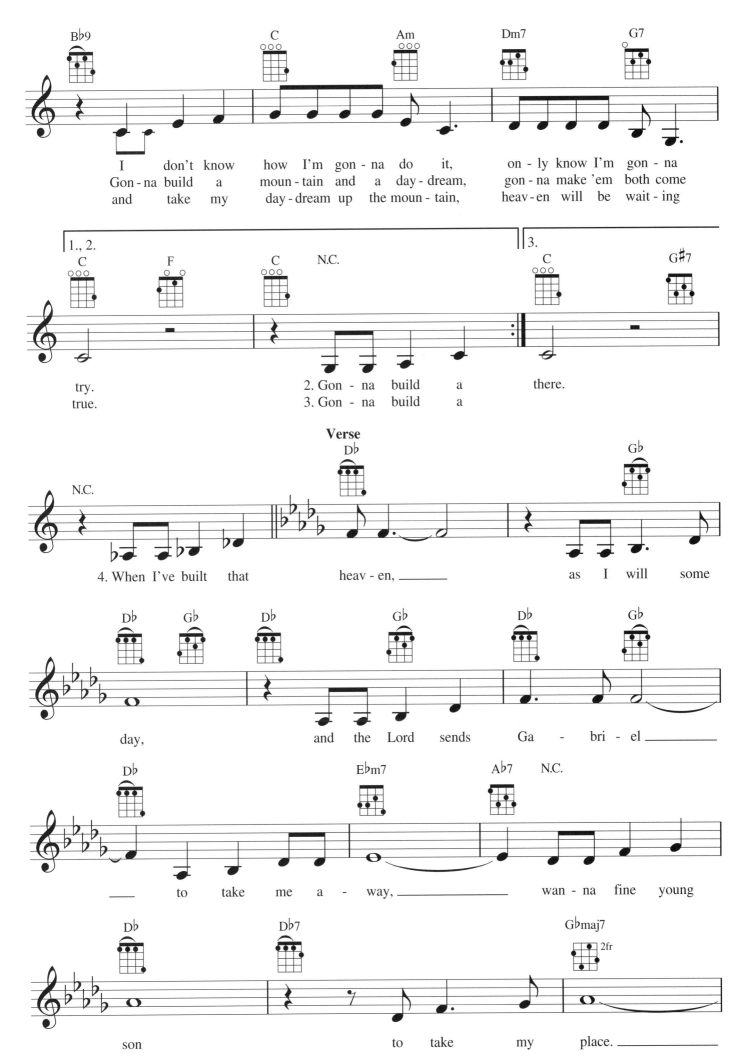

I don't know how I'm gon-na do it,
only know I'm gon-na
Gon-na build a moun-tain and a day-dream,
gon-na make 'em both come
and take my day-dream up the moun-tain,
heav-en will be wait-ing

1., 2.
try.
true.

3.

N.C.
2. Gon - na build a there.
3. Gon - na build a

Verse

N.C.
4. When I've built that heav - en, _____ as I will some

day, and the Lord sends Ga - bri - el _____

_____ to take me a - way, _____ wan - na fine young

son to take my place. _____

Outro

Grandioso

I'll leave a son in my heav-en on earth, with the good _ Lord's grace. With a fine young son to take my place, I'll leave a son in my heav-en on earth with the good Lord's grace. _____

Extra Verses

Gonna build a heaven from a little hell.
Gonna build a heaven, and I know darn well,
With a fine young son to take my place
There'll be a son in my heaven on earth,
With the good Lord's grace.

Gonna build a mountain from a little hill.
Gonna build a mountain—least I hope I will.
Gonna build a mountain—gonna build it high.
I don't know how I'm gonna do it—
Only know I'm gonna try.

Goodnight, My Someone

from Meredith Willson's THE MUSIC MAN
By Meredith Willson

First note

Hello, Dolly!

from HELLO, DOLLY!
Words and Music by Jerry Herman

First note

Chorus
Medium Strut tempo

Hel - lo, Dol - ly, well, hel - lo,

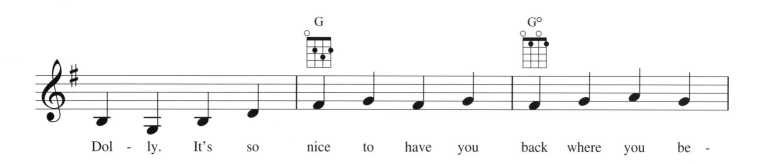

Dol - ly. It's so nice to have you back where you be -

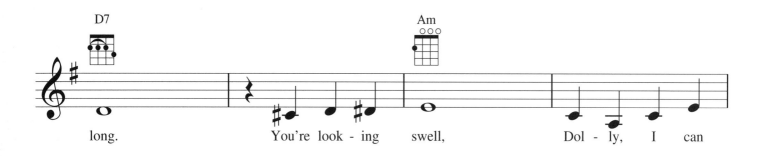

long. You're look - ing swell, Dol - ly, I can

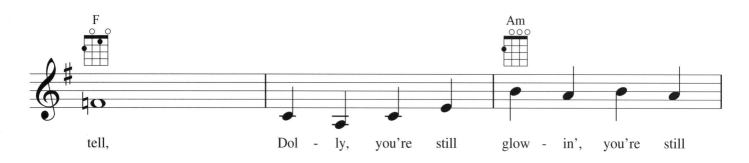

tell, Dol - ly, you're still glow - in', you're still

crow - in', you're still go - in' strong. I feel the

room sway - in' for the band's

play - in' one of your old fav - 'rite songs from way back

Outro

when. So, take her

wrap, fel - las, find her an emp - ty lap, fel - las.

Dol - ly - 'll nev - er go a - way a - gain. _____

Honey Bun

from SOUTH PACIFIC
Lyrics by Oscar Hammerstein II
Music by Richard Rodgers

Bridge

hair is blond and curl - y, her curls are hur - ly

bur - ly. Her lips are pips! ___ I call her hips: ___

Outro-Chorus

"Twirl - y" ___ and "Whirl - y." ___ She's my ba - by,

I'm her pap! ___ I'm her boob - y, she's my trap! ___

I am caught and I don't wan - na run ___ 'cause I'm hav - in' so much

fun with hon - ey - bun! ___

I Can't Give You Anything But Love

from BLACKBIRDS OF 1928
Words and Music by Jimmy McHugh
and Dorothy Fields

First note

Chorus
Snappy

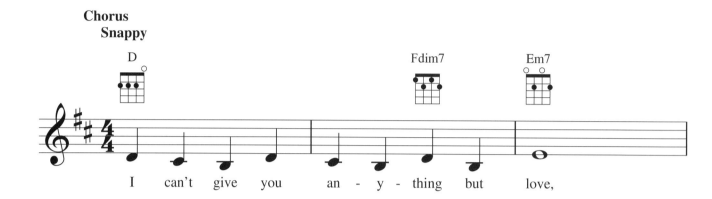

I can't give you an-y-thing but love,

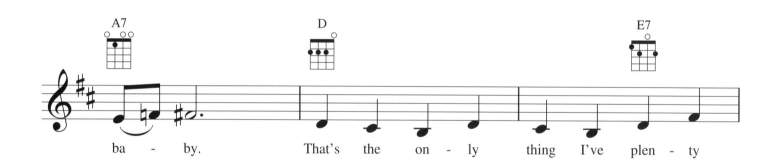

ba - by. That's the on - ly thing I've plen - ty

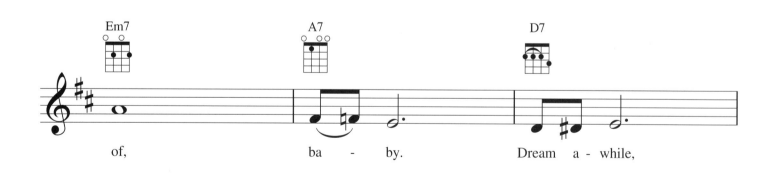

of, ba - by. Dream a - while,

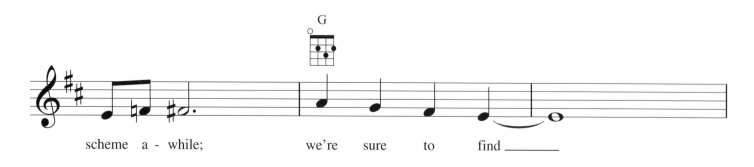

scheme a - while; we're sure to find _____

hap - pi - ness, and I guess all those things you've

al - ways pined for. Gee, I'd like to see you look - ing

swell, ba - by. Dia - mond brace - lets

Wool - worth does - n't sell, ba - by.

'Til that luck - y day, you know darned well, ba - by,

I can't give you an - y - thing but love. _____

I Whistle a Happy Tune

from THE KING AND I
Lyrics by Oscar Hammerstein II
Music by Richard Rodgers

Bridge

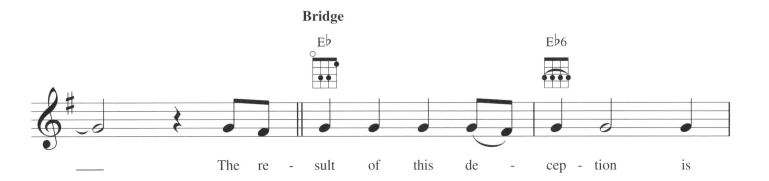

_____ The re - sult of this de - cep - tion is

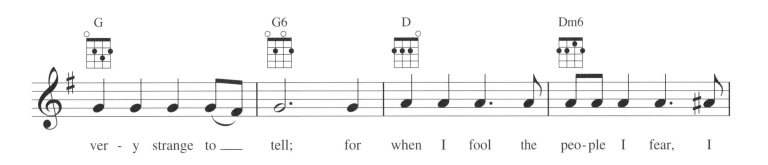

ver - y strange to ___ tell; for when I fool the peo-ple I fear, I

Chorus

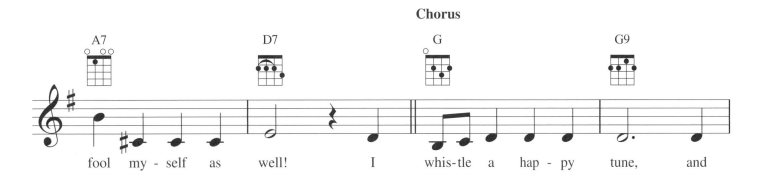

fool my - self as well! I whis-tle a hap-py tune, and

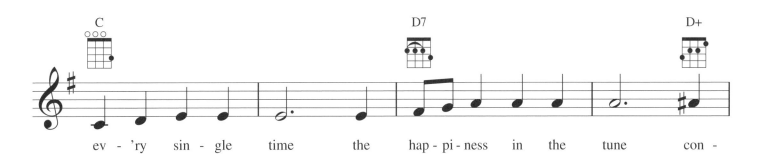

ev - 'ry sin - gle time the hap - pi - ness in the tune con -

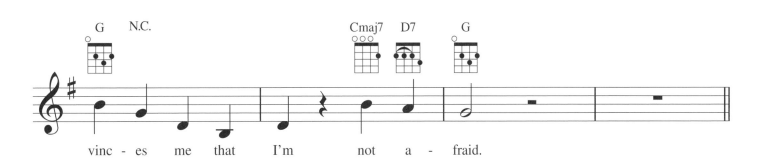

vinc - es me that I'm not a - fraid.

Coda

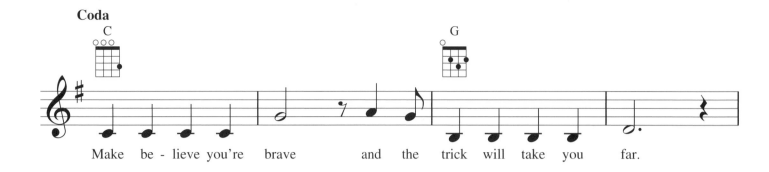

Make be - lieve you're brave and the trick will take you far.

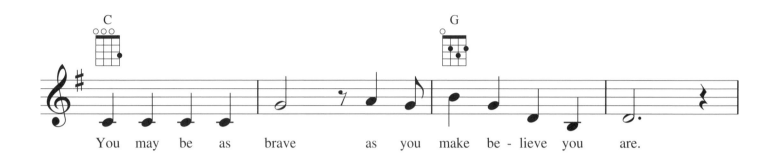

You may be as brave as you make be - lieve you are.

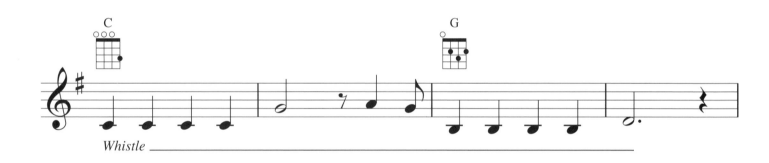

Whistle _____

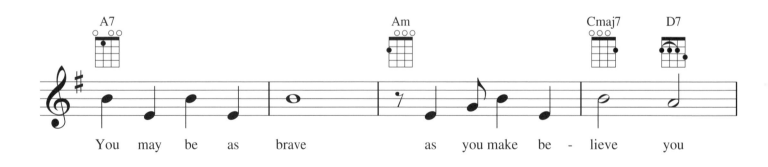

You may be as brave as you make be - lieve you

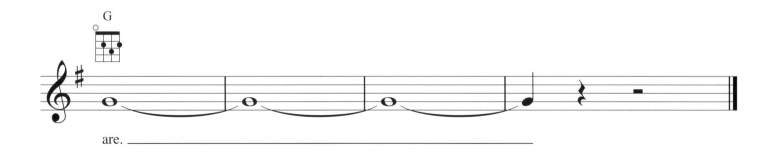

are. _____

If I Were a Rich Man

from the Musical FIDDLER ON THE ROOF
Words by Sheldon Harnick
Music by Jerry Bock

wife with a prop-er dou-ble chin, su-per-vis-ing

meals to her heart's de-light. I see her

put-ting on airs and strut-ting like a pea-cock. Oy! What a hap-py mood she's

in, scream-ing at the ser-vants day and

Interlude-Recitative
Rubato
N.C.

night. The most im-por-tant men in

town will come to fawn on ___ me; they will ask me to ad-vise them,

like a Sol-o-mon the wise. "If you please, Reb Tev-ye, par-don me, Reb Tev-ye,"

pos-ing prob-lems that would cross a rab-bi's eyes. Boi, boi, boi, boi, boi, boi, boi, boi, boi. __

Deliberately (in tempo)

And it won't make one bit of dif-f'rence if I an-swer right or

wrong. When you're rich, they think you real - ly

know. If I were rich, I'd have the

time that I lack to sit in the syn-a-gogue and pray and

Dm7 — **G7** — **C**

may - be have a seat by the east - ern wall.

C7 — **Fm7** — **Bb7**

And I'd dis - cuss the ho - ly books with the learn - ed

Ebmaj7 *3fr* — **Gm7b5** **C7** **Fm**

men sev - en ho - urs ev - 'ry day: this would be the

F#dim7 — **G7**

sweet - est thing of all. _____ *(Sigh)*

Chorus
Tempo I

C

If I were a rich man, dai - dle, dee - dle, dai - dle,

dig - guh, dig - guh, dee - dle, dai - dle, dum,

all day long I'd   bid - dy, bid - dy bum,   if I were a wealth - y

man.   Would-n't have to work hard,   dai - dle, dee - dle, dai - dle,

Outro
Rubato

dig - guh, dig - guh, dee - dle, dai - dle,   dum.   Lord,   who   made   the

li - on   and   the   lamb,   You   de - creed   I   should   be   what   I   am.

Would   it   spoil   some   vast   e - ter - nal   plan   if   I   were   a   wealth - y

Tempo I

man? _____

If I Were a Bell

from GUYS AND DOLLS
By Frank Loesser

Look for the Silver Lining

from SALLY
Words by Buddy DeSylva
Music by Jerome Kern

Makin' Whoopee!

from WHOOPEE!
Lyrics by Gus Kahn
Music by Walter Donaldson

First note

Chorus
Moderately

2., 4.

Em7　　　A7　　　B♭7　　　A7

2. A　lot　of　will - ing _____ to make
4. She　sits　a - "Is　he?" _____ He's mak - in'

Bridge

D　　　　Adim7

whoop - ee!　　　Pic - ture　a　lit - tle
whoop - ee!　　　He　does - n't make much

Em　　　Gm6

love - nest　　　down where　the　ros - es
mon - ey,　　　on - ly　five　thou - sand

D　　　Adim7

cling.　　　Pic - ture　the　same　sweet
per.　　　Some　judge　who　thinks　he's

Em　　　Gm6

love - nest;　　　think　what　a　year　can
fun - ny　　　says, "You'll　pay　six　to

Is You Is, Or Is You Ain't
(Ma' Baby)

from FIVE GUYS NAMED MOE

**Words and Music by Billy Austin
and Louis Jordan**

when you're sure of one, you find {she's / he's} gone and made a change. —

Chorus

— Is you is, or is you ain't ma' ba-

- by? May-be ba-by's

found some-bod-y new, _____ or

1.
is ma' ba-by still ma' ba-by true? ____

2.
still ma' ba-by true? _____

Mame

from MAME

Music and Lyric by Jerry Herman

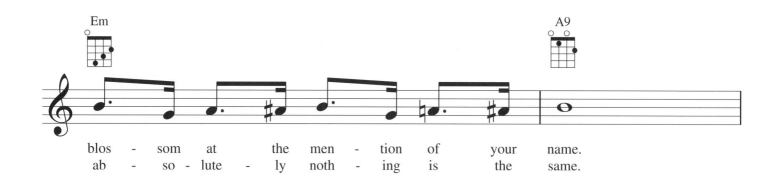

blos - som at the men - tion of your name.
ab - so - lute - ly noth - ing is the same.

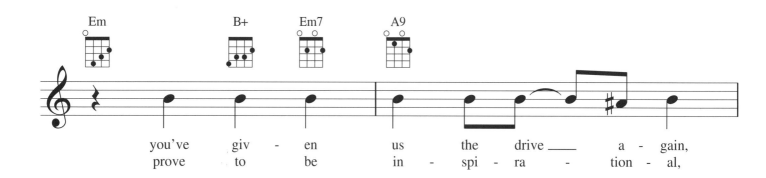

You've made us feel a - live _____ a - gain,
Your spe - cial fas - ci - na - tion - 'll

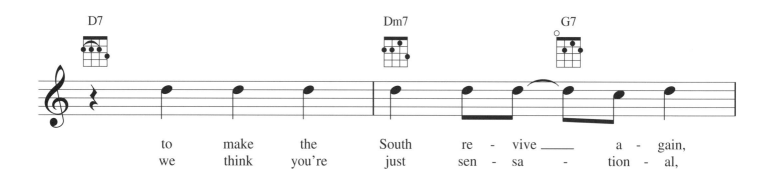

you've giv - en us the drive _____ a - gain,
prove to be in - spi - ra - tion - al,

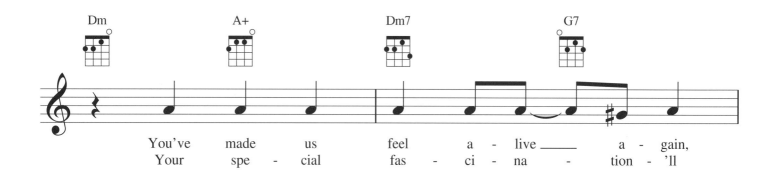

to make the South re - vive _____ a - gain,
we think you're just sen - sa - tion - al,

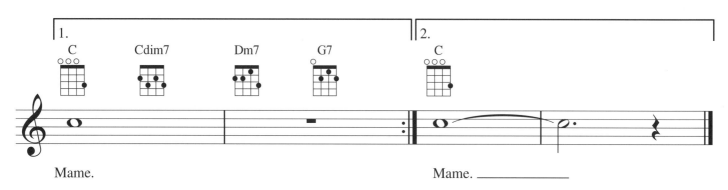

1.
Mame.

2.
Mame. _____

Me and My Girl

from ME AND MY GIRL

Music by Noel Gay
Words by Arthur Rose and Douglas Furber

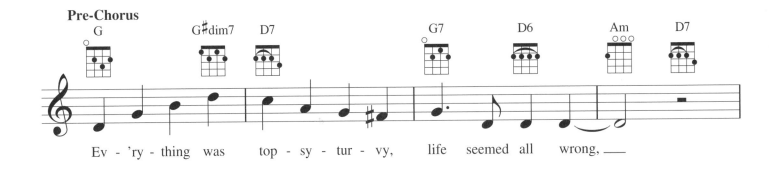

Ev - 'ry - thing was top - sy - tur - vy, life seemed all wrong, ___

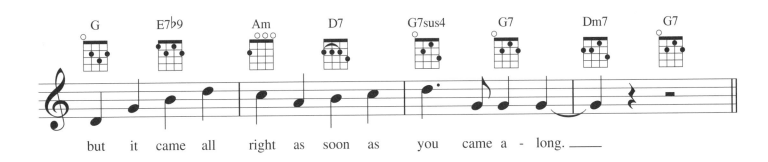

but it came all right as soon as you came a - long. ___

Chorus
Relaxed two-beat

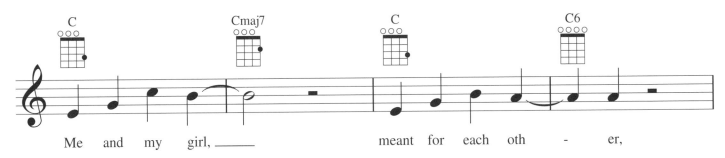

Me and my girl, ___ meant for each oth - er,

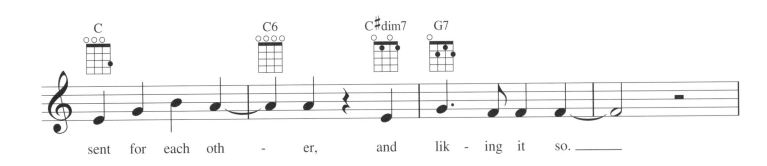

sent for each oth - er, and lik - ing it so. ___

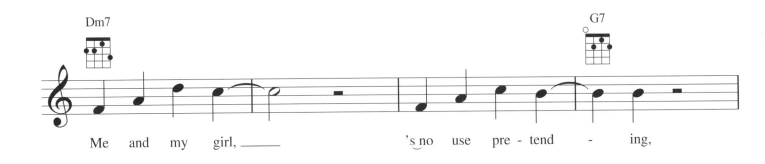

Me and my girl, ___ 's no use pre - tend - ing,

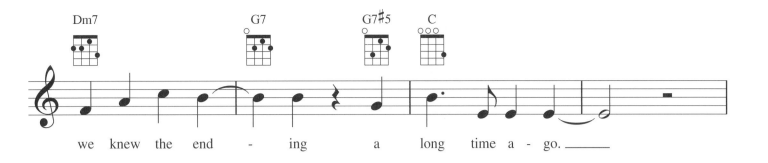

we knew the end - ing   a   long   time a - go. _____

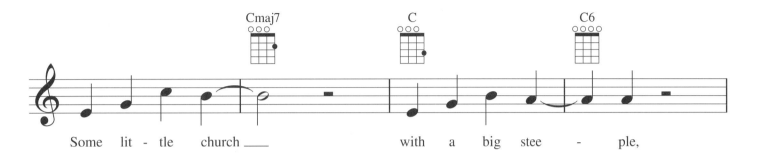

Some lit - tle church _____   with   a   big stee - ple,

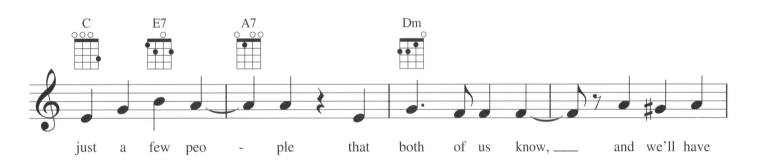

just a few peo - ple   that   both   of us know, ___   and we'll have

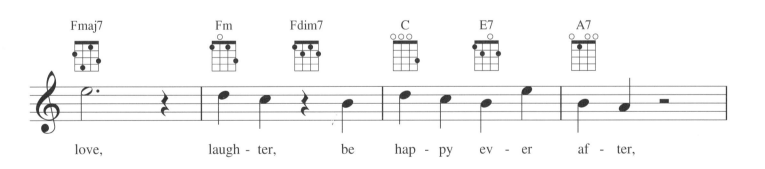

love,   laugh - ter,   be   hap - py ev - er af - ter,

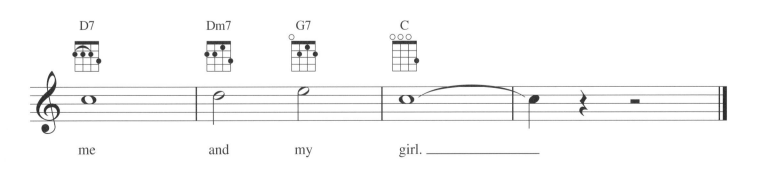

me   and   my   girl. _____

Matchmaker

from the Musical FIDDLER ON THE ROOF
Words by Sheldon Harnick
Music by Jerry Bock

Bring me a ring, for I'm long-ing to be the
Up to this min-ute, I mis-un-der-stood that

en-vy of all I see. _____ For
I could get all stuck for good. _____ Dear

Bridge

Pop - pa, make him a schol-ar, for Mom -
Mom - ma, see that he's gen-tle. Re - mem -

To Coda ⊕

ma, make him rich as a king. For me, well,
ber, you were al-so a bride. It's

I would-n't hol-ler if he were as hand-some as

Chorus

an - y - thing. Match-mak-er, match-mak-er, make me a

67

match, find me a find, catch me a catch;

Night af - ter night in the dark I'm a - lone, so

find me a match of my own. _____

D.S. al Coda

Coda

not that

I'm sen - ti - men - tal. It's just that I'm

Chorus

ter - ri - fied! _____ Match - mak - er,

match - mak - er,   plan   me   no   plans;   I'm   in   no

rush,   may - be   I've   learned   play - ing   with   match - es   a

Outro

girl   can   get   burned.   So   bring   me   no   ring,   groom   me   no

groom,   find   me   no   find,   catch   me   no   catch,

un - less   he's   a   match - less

match! _____

Never Never Land

from PETER PAN
Lyric by Betty Comden and Adolph Green
Music by Jule Styne

Bridge

Land. You'll have a treas - ure if you stay there,

more pre - cious far than gold. For once you have found your

way there, you can nev - er, nev - er grow old. So

Verse

come with me where dreams are born, and time is nev - er

planned. Just think of love - ly things, and your heart will fly on wings, for

Outro

ev - er in Nev - er Nev - er Land. _____

71

Once in Love with Amy

from WHERE'S CHARLEY?

By Frank Loesser

Tomorrow

from the Musical Production ANNIE
Lyric by Martin Charnin
Music by Charles Strouse

lone - ly, I just stick — out my chin and grin and

Chorus

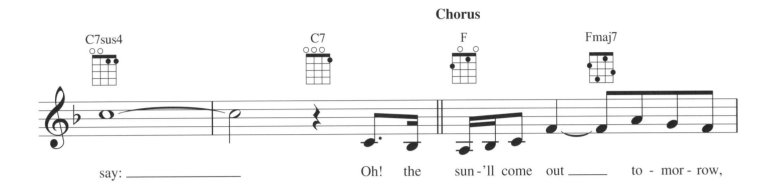

say: _____ Oh! the sun - 'll come out ____ to - mor - row,

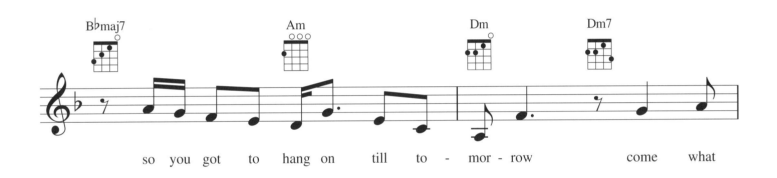

so you got to hang on till to - mor - row come what

Outro

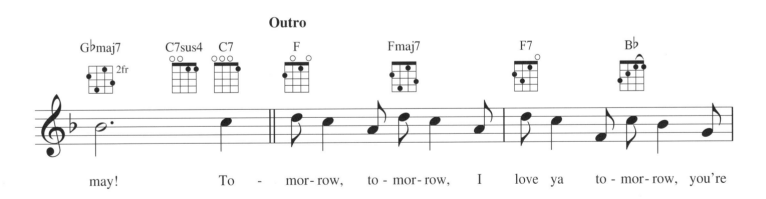

may! To - mor - row, to - mor - row, I love ya to - mor - row, you're

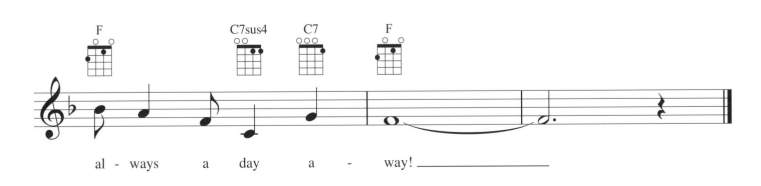

al - ways a day a - way! _____

Once Upon a Time

from the Broadway Musical ALL AMERICAN
Lyric by Lee Adams
Music by Charles Strouse

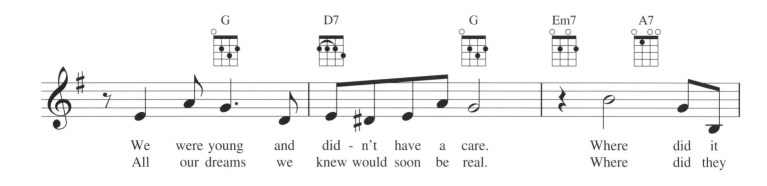

We were young and did - n't have a care.
All our dreams we knew would soon be real. Where did it

Where did they

Outro-Chorus

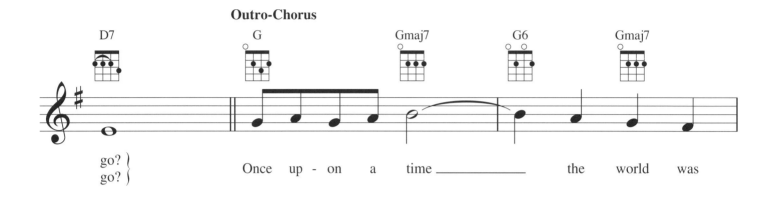

go?
go? Once up - on a time _____ the world was

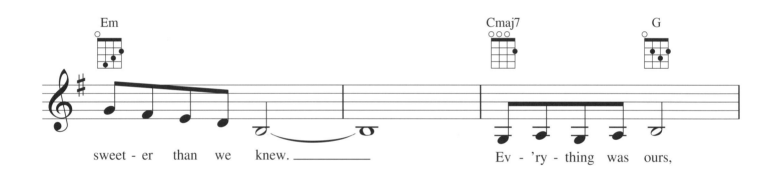

sweet - er than we knew. _____ Ev - 'ry - thing was ours,

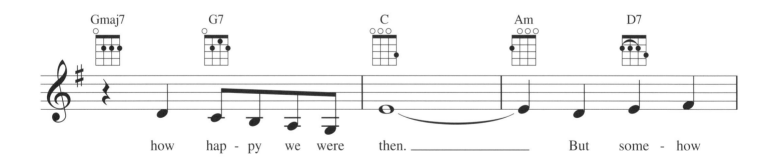

how hap - py we were then. _____ But some - how

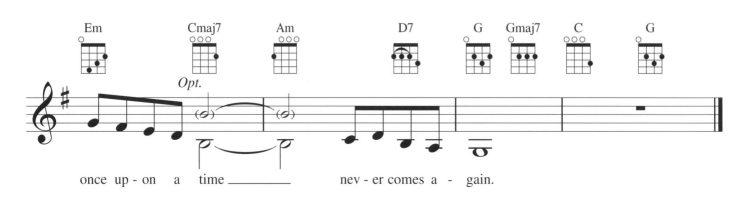

Opt.

once up - on a time _____ nev - er comes a - gain.

HAL•LEONARD UKULELE PLAY-ALONG®

1. POP HITS
American Pie • Copacabana (At the Copa) • Crocodile Rock • Kokomo • Lean on Me • Stand by Me • Twist and Shout • What the World Needs Now Is Love.
00701451 Book/CD Pack.............$14.99

2. UKE CLASSICS
Ain't She Sweet • Five Foot Two, Eyes of Blue (Has Anybody Seen My Girl?) • It's Only a Paper Moon • Living in the Sunlight, Loving in the Moonlight • Pennies from Heaven • Tonight You Belong to Me • Ukulele Lady • When I'm Cleaning Windows.
00701452 Book/CD Pack.............$12.99

3. HAWAIIAN FAVORITES
Aloha Oe • Blue Hawaii • Harbor Lights • The Hawaiian Wedding Song (Ke Kali Nei Au) • Mele Kalikimaka • Sleepy Lagoon • Sweet Someone • Tiny Bubbles.
00701453 Book/CD Pack.............$12.99

4. CHILDREN'S SONGS
Do-Re-Mi • The Hokey Pokey • It's a Small World • My Favorite Things • Puff the Magic Dragon • Sesame Street Theme • Splish Splash • This Land Is Your Land.
00701454 Book/CD Pack.............$12.99

5. CHRISTMAS SONGS `INCLUDES TAB`
Do You Hear What I Hear • Feliz Navidad • Frosty the Snow Man • Here Comes Santa Claus (Right down Santa Claus Lane) • Jingle-Bell Rock • Nuttin' for Christmas • Rudolph the Red-Nosed Reindeer • Santa Claus Is Comin' to Town.
00701696 Book/CD Pack.............$12.99

6. LENNON & McCARTNEY
And I Love Her • Day Tripper • Here, There and Everywhere • Hey Jude • Let It Be • Norwegian Wood (This Bird Has Flown) • Nowhere Man • Yesterday.
00701723 Book/CD Pack.............$12.99

7. DISNEY FAVORITES
Alice in Wonderland • The Bare Necessities • Candle on the Water • Chim Chim Cher-ee • A Dream Is a Wish Your Heart Makes • Mickey Mouse March • Supercalifragilisticexpialidocious • Under the Sea.
00701724 Book/CD Pack.............$12.99

8. CHART HITS
All the Right Moves • Bubbly • Hey, Soul Sister • I'm Yours • Toes • Use Somebody • Viva la Vida • You're Beautiful.
00701745 Book/CD Pack.............$12.99

9. THE SOUND OF MUSIC
Climb Ev'ry Mountain • Do-Re-Mi • Edelweiss • Maria • My Favorite Things • Sixteen Going on Seventeen • Something Good • The Sound of Music.
00701784 Book/CD Pack.............$12.99

11. CHRISTMAS STRUMMING
Away in a Manger • Deck the Hall • The First Noel • Hark! the Herald Angels Sing • Jingle Bells • Joy to the World • O Come, All Ye Faithful (Adeste Fideles) • We Three Kings of Orient Are.
00702458 Book/CD Pack.............$12.99

13. UKULELE SONGS
Daughter • Dream a Little Dream of Me • Elderly Woman Behind the Counter in a Small Town • Last Kiss • More Than You Know • Sleepless Nights • Tonight You Belong to Me • Yellow Ledbetter.
00702599 Book/CD Pack.............$12.99

FOR MORE INFORMATION, SEE YOUR LOCAL MUSIC DEALER, OR WRITE TO:

HAL•LEONARD® CORPORATION
7777 W. BLUEMOUND RD. P.O. BOX 13819 MILWAUKEE, WI 53213

www.halleonard.com

Prices, contents, and availability subject to change without notice.
Disney characters and artwork © Disney Enterprises, Inc.

Ride the Ukulele Wave!

The Beach Boys for Ukulele

This folio features 20 favorites, including: Barbara Ann • Be True to Your School • California Girls • Fun, Fun, Fun • God Only Knows • Good Vibrations • Help Me Rhonda • I Get Around • In My Room • Kokomo • Little Deuce Coupe • Sloop John B • Surfin' U.S.A. • Wouldn't It Be Nice • and more!

00701726 . . . . $14.99

Disney Songs for Ukulele

20 great Disney classics arranged for all uke players, including: Beauty and the Beast • Bibbidi-Bobbidi-Boo (The Magic Song) • Can You Feel the Love Tonight • Chim Chim Cher-ee • Heigh-Ho • It's a Small World • Some Day My Prince Will Come • We're All in This Together • When You Wish upon a Star • and more.

00701708 . . . . $12.99

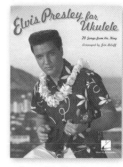

Elvis Presley for Ukulele

arr. Jim Beloff

20 classic hits from The King: All Shook Up • Blue Hawaii • Blue Suede Shoes • Can't Help Falling in Love • Don't • Heartbreak Hotel • Hound Dog • Jailhouse Rock • Love Me • Love Me Tender • Return to Sender • Suspicious Minds • Teddy Bear • and more.

00701004 . . . . $14.99

The Beatles for Ukulele

Ukulele players can strum, sing and pick along with 20 Beatles classics! Includes: All You Need Is Love • Eight Days a Week • Good Day Sunshine • Here, There and Everywhere • Let It Be • Love Me Do • Penny Lane • Yesterday • and more.

00700154 . . . . $16.99

Folk Songs for Ukulele

A great collection to take along to the campfire! 60 folk songs, including: Amazing Grace • Buffalo Gals • Camptown Races • For He's a Jolly Good Fellow • Good Night Ladies • Home on the Range • I've Been Working on the Railroad • Kumbaya • My Bonnie Lies over the Ocean • On Top of Old Smoky • Scarborough Fair • Swing Low, Sweet Chariot • Take Me Out to the Ball Game • Yankee Doodle • and more.

00696068 . . . . $12.99

Hawaiian Songs for Ukulele

Over thirty songs from the state that made the ukulele famous, including: Beyond the Rainbow • Hanalei Moon • Ka-lu-a • Lovely Hula Girl • Mele Kalikimaka • One More Aloha • Sea Breeze • Tiny Bubbles • Waikiki • and more.

00696065 . . . . $9.99

Irving Berlin Songs Arranged for the "Uke"

20 great songs with full instructions, including: Always • Blue Skies • Easter Parade • How Deep Is the Ocean (How High Is the Sky) • A Pretty Girl Is like a Melody • Say It with Music • What'll I Do? • White Christmas • and more.

00005558 . . . . $6.95

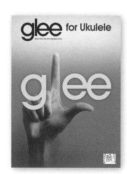

Glee

Music from the Fox Television Show for Ukulele

20 favorites for Gleeks to strum and sing, including: Bad Romance • Beautiful • Defying Gravity • Don't Stop Believin' • No Air • Proud Mary • Rehab • True Colors • and more.

00701722 . . . $14.99

Worship Songs for Ukulele

25 worship songs: Amazing Grace (My Chains are Gone) • Blessed Be Your Name • Enough • God of Wonders • Holy Is the Lord • How Great Is Our God • In Christ Alone • I Love the Lord • Mighty to Save • Sing to the King • Step by Step • We Fall Down • and more.

00702546 . . . . $12.99

The Daily Ukulele

compiled and arranged by

Liz and Jim Beloff

Strum a different song everyday with easy arrangements of 365 of your favorite songs in one big songbook! Includes favorites by the Beatles, Beach Boys, and Bob Dylan, folk songs, pop songs, kids' songs, Christmas carols, and Broadway and Hollywood tunes, all with a spiral binding for ease of use.

00240356 . . . . $34.99

Jake Shimabukuro – Peace Love Ukulele

Deemed "the Hendrix of the ukulele," Hawaii native Jake Shimabukuro is a uke virtuoso. Our songbook features note-for-note transcriptions with ukulele tablature of Jake's masterful playing on all the CD tracks: Bohemian Rhapsody • Boy Meets Girl • Bring Your Adz • Hallelujah • Pianoforte 2010 • Variation on a Dance 2010 • and more, plus two bonus selections!

00702516 . . . . $19.99

Rodgers & Hammerstein for Ukulele

arr. Jim Beloff

Now you can play 20 classic show tunes from this beloved songwriting duo on your uke! Includes: All at Once You Love Her • Do-Re-Mi • Edelweiss • Getting to Know You • Impossible • My Favorite Things • and more.

00701905 . . . . $12.99

HAL•LEONARD CORPORATION
7777 W. BLUEMOUND RD. P.O. BOX 13819 MILWAUKEE, WI 5321

02